# Jen Bu

by Shirley Frederick

illustrations by Tuko Fujisaki

**Harcourt Brace & Company**
Orlando  Atlanta  Austin  Boston  San Francisco  Chicago  Dallas  New York  Toronto  London

Jennifer Tuttle is taking a bath.
The water begins to bubble.
Jennifer lets the water run.
Oh, oh! Here comes trouble!

Playing so happily in the tub,
Jennifer isn't aware
That bubbles, like marbles round and bright,
Will tumble everywhere!

Jennifer adds some bubble soap.
Jennifer adds some more!
She doesn't see bubbles run
   over the tub

And out of the bathroom door!

A river of bubbles is off
   and away,
Over and under the table.
Bubbles sweep away all
   of the dirt.
Bubbles flow where they
   are able.

"Bubbles tickle!" says little Anna.
She bats them away with glee.
Anna giggles. "Bubbles are fun!"
Her father doesn't agree!

Bubbles ripple along the street
To the home of Lester Hubble.
Lester Hubble calls 9-1-1.

The firefighters set out on the double.

Fisher Bumble hollers, "Ahoy!"
In a voice as loud as thunder.
"The bubbles flow all around—
About, in the middle, and
   under!"

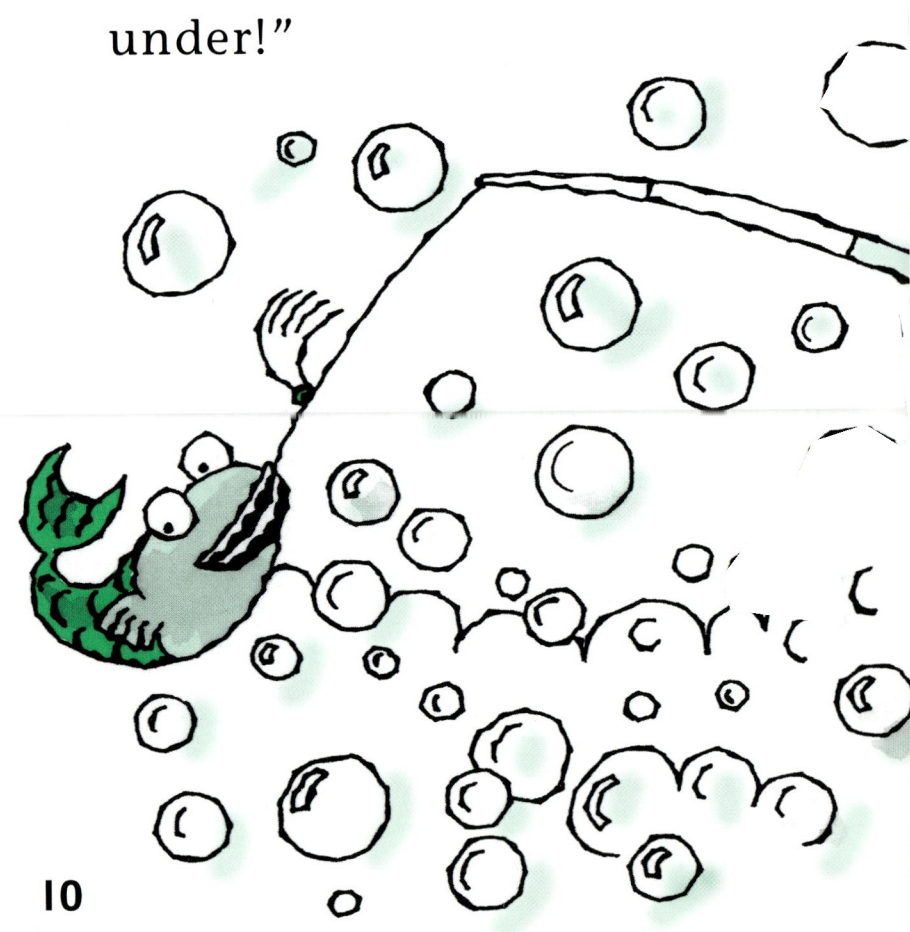

Chester Tuttle is quite amazed
At his little sister's lather.
"Jennifer Tuttle!" he cries
 in alarm.
 "Just wait till I tell Mother!"

"Mother!" says Chester.
"Something's amiss! Hurry!
You must come and see!"
So they stumble amid the
bubbles—
Oh, where can Jennifer be?

"Jennifer!" Mother grumbles.
"Jennifer Tuttle, what have
 you done?
We're being attacked by bubbles!
And this isn't any fun!"

Then Jennifer Tuttle's mother,
Adrift in a bubble sea,
Chuckles and says to Chester,
"This IS fun! Don't you agree?"

Jennifer turns the water off.
The bubbles soon fade away.
She'll dabble her duck in the waves awhile—
The bathtub's a great place to play!